RAISED
FROM THE DEAD

Brugada Syndrome Survivor
"Seven (7%) Percenter"

BY
LAWRENCE E. HODGES

Exulon
Elite

Copyright © 2015 by Lawrence E. Hodges

Raised From The Dead
Brugada Syndrome Survivor "Seven (7%) Percenter"
by Lawrence E. Hodges

Printed in the United States of America.

ISBN 9781498458283

All rights reserved solely by the author. The author guarantees all contents are original and do not infringe upon the legal rights of any other person or work. No part of this book may be reproduced in any form without the permission of the author. The views expressed in this book are not necessarily those of the publisher.

Scripture quotations taken from the King James Version (KJV) – *public domain*

Author Disclaimer:
This book is based on true-life events. I have tried to recreate events, locales and conversations from both my memories and that of others. In order to maintain the privacy of all parties involved some names and identifying details have been changed to protect the privacy of those individuals

www.xulonpress.com

ACKNOWLEDGEMENTS

First of all, I thank my Lord and Savior, Jesus Christ, for the privilege and honor to even be able to write this book. Secondly, I thank all my church members for their love and support—100 percent! I thank my Mother, Mrs. Dana Grubb, Greg Grubb, Mrs. Barbara Gilbreath, Tommy Gilbreath, Diana Walla, Mrs. Andrea Booth, Randy Booth, Mrs. Sandi Propst, and Dr. Wayne Propst, the staff at the Bethesda Health Clinic. And, I also thank all the rest of the Glenwood Church of Christ for all your faithful prayers and love. Let it be known that just because I didn't mention your name in this letter doesn't mean I don't recognize or acknowledge you, but rather, I might not remember your name or it wasn't meant to be mentioned. God knows your heart, and He, Jesus Christ, will reward you for your good works and deeds done here on this earth. Amen! I love you, Glenwood!

Lawrence Hodges

INTRODUCTION

I, Lawrence E. Hodges, felt led by the Holy Spirit to write a book about my life, as an autobiography. I felt the Lord Jesus Christ has been sustaining my life for this purpose. I believe this is one of the ways that the LORD is using my life, to bring Himself glory. The Lord has shown me mercy and forgiveness in many ways. God's nature and attributes are pure and holy. Let it be known <u>this</u> <u>day</u>, this book is <u>only</u> written to bring glory, praise and honor to the name "Jesus." The name above every name under heaven (Acts 4:12). Whatever you do, do all to the glory of God. (1 Cor. 10:31) (Col. 3:23). I believe and hope the believers will enjoy this book to the fullest and be blessed by it ultimately. In addition, I hope the unsaved will become saved after reading my story about Jesus Christ. Jesus Christ is the only way to the Father (John 14:6). The Lord desires for none to perish but that all may come to the knowledge of the truth. (1 Tim. 2:4) (2 Pet. 3:9)

I would like to personally thank and commend Mrs. Dana Grubb and Barbara Gilbreath for their love, support and encouragement in preparing this book. I also would like to thank Mrs. Patricia (Pat) Mallory for recommending me to Xulon Press to get my book published.

Lawrence E. Hodges

PREFACE

I have Brugada Syndrome, a very rare heart rhythm disorder. Only five out of 10,000 people worldwide acquire this generally unknown disease. It was first discovered in Southeast Asia. I just happened to be in this very small percentage. There is <u>no medication</u> whatsoever for this deadly disease. The only treatment for this heart disorder is a medical device which is a defibrillator or pacemaker. Brugada Syndrome is oftentimes genetic, but it can be acquired over the years when there is no family history. Only 7 percent of the people survive this heart attack because the other 93 percent don't have a defibrillator available at the time of the attack. Therefore, they die instantly. Brugada Syndrome is sometimes called "sudden death." It's like a nightmare and a sudden death sentence all at once. Brugada Syndrome is not like many diseases and/or chronic illnesses and disorders, such as diabetes, high blood pressure, leukemia, sickle cell anemia, or some cancers. You may live with these sicknesses months and even years. That is not so with Brugada Syndrome. The day it becomes dynamic in your body, it can take your life—<u>the very same day it becomes active in your body</u>! You may die because it instantly stops your heart from beating altogether.

TABLE OF CONTENTS

Chapter 1 – Many Eyewitnesses 13

Chapter 2 – Testimony of a Thankful Patient 37

Chapter 3 – Spiritual Warfare 43

Chapter 4 – Physical and Emotional
              Struggles with BPPV 47

Chapter 5 – My Beginning 53

Chapter 6 – Taking and Breaking 59

Chapter 7 – How Will It All End? 93

Chapter 1

MANY EYEWITNESSES

"Numbers, what do they mean?"

(Acts 9:36 - 41)

Now, numbers don't generally mean anything in particular on a day to day basis, however, this was a DIVINE day. Any divine day is a special day when God is doing something extraordinary. This particular day, God had set aside to resurrect me. I died a physical death on September 26, 2013, and Jesus Christ resurrected me after I was dead for fifteen minutes. A notable miracle!! Jesus Christ sent my breath back into my body after fifteen minutes of no breathing whatsoever. What I suggest is: anyone who desires to learn more about numbers in the Bible and how Jesus Christ uses them to speak to us should do a Google search on the number(s) you're seeking, then take that information to the Bible and learn how Jesus Christ used the number(s). Perhaps you have a divine situation that occurred in your life, and you desire to know what Jesus Christ is speaking to you. Ask the Holy Spirit and He will reveal all truth to you. Just let the Holy Spirit do His job—that's part of His duties.

"DIVINE NUMBERS" that were existing on that divine and special day!

The numbers below were all existing on the day I died and was resurrected. I prayed and Googled them, and found that they are all associated with God in the Bible.

#7   #15   #26   #44

Number 7 means <u>completion</u> in the Bible. Dr. Simms, the heart surgeon who put in my defibrillator, said that I am a 7 percenter, meaning that only 7 percent of the people who are attacked by Brugada Syndrome survive.

Number 15 means <u>rest</u> in the Bible and is connected to the resurrection. I was dead fifteen minutes and Jesus Christ resurrected me.

The number 26 is a number for a holy and righteous God. More especially, #26 seems a number purely about God and Jesus. My heart attack occurred on September 26, 2013.

Number 44 is the number of "chosen people." I am forty-four years old and this is how it all began.

MY EYEWITNESS ACCOUNT OF EVENTS

Tuesday morning was the initial day that I was attacked by Brugada Syndrome. I awoke from my night's sleep as I always do and got out of bed. I took a couple of steps and began to black out. I intentionally fell toward my couch so I wouldn't hit the floor. I remained on my couch for a few moments to regain my stability and balance. While I was on the couch, I was asking myself, "What is this? I don't have high blood pressure or diabetes. I only take medication for my left wrist and that is just inflammation pills, Naproxen, and they wouldn't do this."

Finally, I began to make slow and cautious steps, getting up after my fall or blackout. I used my couch side arms to elevate myself. I got up and took baby steps to the kitchen where I was initially headed. I think I ate breakfast. I left to go to my mother's house. I stayed there until I got a phone call from my dump truck supervisor. He said to come over and ride with him. We needed to discuss the problem that occurred at the dump truck job the Friday before. I told him I was on my way.

I got to the shop and we left in my dump truck for the wrecking yard. We discussed the matter about the issue at the last job site. I told him all that had happened and we resolved it afterwards. We got to the wrecking yard and found the part we needed to weld on the back of my truck for pulling vehicles out of mud and holes. My boss discussed it with the guy who would order it to be cut off one of his trucks. My boss and I then left after about two hours and went back to the shop.

He said, "I'll call you when I hear something about work." I said, "Okay." I then left to go home to eat a late lunch before going to my next job at Einstein Bros. Bagels, to do scrubbing and cleaning. I arrived there at 5:00 PM. I worked for three hours and clocked out at 8:00 PM. I told Ray Fletcher, my general manager, that I was done.

He said, "Thanks, Lawrence! See you when I see you!" I said, "Okay," and left.

I went back home Tuesday night, got on the phone, brushed my teeth and went to sleep. I awoke Wednesday morning and got out of bed with no problem. I ate breakfast and went to Gateway to Hope on Valentine Street to get on the Internet, looking for a truck driving job. I found a few, and I left. I went to Mom Deborah's house for lunch. I was there for a short while, and I left. I told her that I would be back that night for supper and church. She said, "Okay." She gave me a hug, and I left. I ran around for a while, and then I went home to get a shower and get ready for church. I went to Mom Deborah's house again.

Mom Deborah and I were waiting on Thomas to arrive to eat with us, but he phoned and said, "Go ahead; I'm running late." So, we ate. He finally came in when we

Raised From The Dead

were leaving the table. Mom Deborah went to brush her teeth; Thomas took his food downstairs to eat in his office, and I got on Mom Deborah's computer for a short minute.

Mom Deborah came out and said, "Well, I'm ready." I asked her if she was teaching the kids tonight, and she said, "Yes." I told her that I'd come later, so she left. She got there about ten minutes before I did. I saw her car and went to my new class on spiritual warfare. We had a good lesson that night. I met Mom Deborah after class, and we walked out together.

She said, "I'll see you later."

I said, "Okay, Mom Deborah." Then I told her to wait a minute. "Mom Deborah, you need to get your headlight fixed." She agreed to do so. She left, and I left too.

I was headed to my Mama's house when I remembered that I forgot the biscuits at Mom Deborah's house. I have been blessed in my life with a wonderful birth mother, but God also sent me a spiritual mom to guide me here on earth, which is my Mom Deborah. She has always been there to take me to church and to help me understand about God. I called Mom Deborah about them. She brought them out and jokingly threw them in my car. I went by my Mama's house afterwards. I parked in the driveway; I got out and went to the porch. I saw that my mother and brother, Harold were probably asleep, but my brother,

Many Eyewitnesses

Jacob, was watching DVD movies. I decided not to disturb him, so I left.

I got to my house Wednesday night, and I think I got on the phone, brushed my teeth, and went to sleep early. I had on my mind to go to Einstein Bros. Bagels in the morning, so I went to sleep early. It was around 9:00 PM. I slept all night without interruption. I awoke early Thursday morning, around 6:00 AM. I got out of bed and went to the bathroom for a minute to use the restroom and wash my face. I ate breakfast. I started to go on a calling spree about what had happened on Tuesday morning. My sister, Wendy was the first person that I called. She didn't answer the phone. My boss from the dump truck job, Travis, called me.

He said, "I surprised you this morning!" I said, "Yeah!" He said, "We don't have any work today, but as soon as we get something, I will call you." I said, "Appreciate your calling. Okay, thanks!" He said, "Take care." I said, "You too. Bye."

I resumed calling. I called my sister-in-law, Sonya, next because she's a nurse, and I had questions for her. She didn't answer the phone.

I fell in my room between 6:30 AM and 6:36 AM. Then, I phoned my real Mama. No one answered the call. I called Mom Deborah again after I called my Mama. Nobody was answering their phone. Then, I called Thomas and he too didn't answer the phone. I called Mom Deborah again. This was my very last phone call. Then, I left my room and went to the parking lot to prepare for going to Mom's house. I got to the parking lot, where I fell again and passed out. That's where I lost my Bluetooth earbud. I got up by the grace of God. I came back in the house to my room to get a yellow sheet of paper to write down the incident that I had just experienced. I became fearful that I might die and nobody would understand what had happened to me that Thursday morning. I felt the need to bring this yellow sheet of paper with me in my car as a detailed list of events that had just occurred with my health. I got in my car and made a left on Goodman Street to Broadway Avenue. I made a right on Broadway and the Angel of the Lord led me to Mom Deborah's house. I arrived there and got out of my car and sat on the porch in the chair closest to the rocking chair. I just calmly sat on the porch. Thomas came back from his morning walk. He recognized me, and he spoke to me, and I spoke back. Thomas asked me what was wrong. I told him that I had fallen in the parking lot at my place, and that I didn't feel well. I was lightheaded and nauseated. Thomas immediately went inside to relay the message to Mom Deborah while I remained on the porch, still confused from the events I had just experienced.

ALL THE PHONE CALLS THAT WERE MADE THE MORNING OF SEPTEMBER 26, 2013 (FROM 6:13 AM UNTIL 7:20 AM)

Eight Outgoing Calls

1st	6:13 AM	Wendy
2nd	6:29 AM	Sister-in-law, Sonya
3rd	6:37 AM	Mama
4th	6:42 AM	Mom Deborah
5th	6:56 AM	Thomas
6th	6:57 AM	Mom Deborah
7th	7:04 AM	Thomas
8th	7:20 AM	Mom Deborah

One Incoming Call

6:16 AM   Travis, my dump truck supervisor, called me concerning work. Travis said, "We don't have anything today, but if anything comes up, I'll let you know." I said, "Okay, thanks for calling me."

Travis was the only person that I talked to by phone Thursday morning. He called a few minutes after I had called my sister, Wendy.

MOM DEBORAH AND THOMAS EYEWITNESSES ACCOUNT OF EVENTS

September 26, 2013

First of all, I respect that you want to know everything that happened that morning. These are my memories, and honestly I'm feeling anxious as I sit here preparing to write them down. It's an awful morning for me to remember. Even though the outcome was that your life was spared, I feel guilty for not taking you directly to the ER! I can still see your lifeless body lying in the parking lot and remember thinking that this could not be happening. So, that said—here goes.

I had just gotten out of bed and was washing my face when Thomas came in the bathroom and said, "Lawrence is sitting on the front porch and wants to talk to you. He says that he doesn't feel good." I could tell that Thomas had been for a walk because he was dressed in shorts and a T-shirt. I said, "What's wrong with him? Why didn't he come in? Did you ask him to come in?" He replied that he didn't know what was wrong, and that when he walked up to the house he could see you sitting in a chair on the porch and that you asked him to go get me.

So I got dressed and went out the front door, feeling sleepy and kind of rattled by the situation. You were sitting in one of the chairs and I walked over to you. You didn't get up or say hello. You just looked up at me and said, "Mom, I don't feel good." When I asked what was wrong, you said that you felt lightheaded and nauseated. At that point, I think Thomas came out with a cookie and something to drink. I believe that he thought you might be having some kind of diabetic episode. Anyway, you kind of waved him away and said you didn't want anything and asked me to take you to the doctor.

Thomas and I just kind of looked at each other, not really understanding what was happening, so I said that I'd go downstairs and bring the car up. I grabbed my purse and phone and came up with the car. I got out of the car and you got up when I came over to you. I think I asked again if you were okay, and then you put your arm around my shoulders and I grabbed your waist and we walked to the car.

I started down Chilton and then turned down Old Jacksonville to Broadway, driving fast. I remember talking to you about where to go—the ER or hospital. I was thinking that you might have a stomach bug and had gotten dehydrated. I was thinking that it was an illness, not having any idea that you were so critical. I was concerned about taking you to the ER and the cost of the ER visit as opposed to a hospital visit. I asked you what you thought and you just said to do whatever I thought was best.

I decided to call Betty to see when the hospital opened, and she told me 8:00. I'm sure we talked about what was going on, but it was a quick conversation. That's when I decided to go to the hospital since it was close to 8:00. I'm sorry I didn't take things more seriously, Lawrence, and I still carry a lot of guilt about that.

I drove quickly and just as we got through the light at Front Street, you started to heave like you were going to throw up. I pulled into the parking lot at The Forum. You opened the door, leaned out, coughed and threw up a little. Mostly dry heaving, I think. You leaned back in and closed the door. That's when I started to feel real fear that something was very wrong. I remember my heart started to pound.

Betty called me either shortly before this happened or slightly after, and when I answered she said that they could see you at 1:00. I think I said that we were way past and I was going straight to the hospital. I'm sure you've talked to her about this timeline. I'm sorry I'm not clearer on that detail.

We drove through a green light at Erwin and I headed to Ferguson. The light was red and there was a car in front of me. Then you started to take these deep, distressing breaths. I just felt panicked because I called your name and you wouldn't answer. Thankfully, the light turned green, and I took off down Ferguson. I ran the red light at College and you started to lean toward me with your left arm on the console. Your breaths became more labored and you grabbed your shirt with your right hand.

I turned into the parking lot at the hospital and pulled into a parking spot. As I recall, you were leaning on the console with your head back. I jumped out of the car and saw a woman walking toward the front door in scrubs. I yelled that I needed help and that there was a man in my car who was passed out. She ran over.

I think I opened the door. She handed me her phone and told me to call 911! So I called immediately and the dispatcher asked what the emergency was. She leaned in and said, "He's not breathing!" My recollection is that she grabbed you and kind of pulled you from the car. You fell backwards and hit the ground with your left leg still in the car.

I was on the phone with the dispatcher, who was very calm and asked me where I was. I remember watching what was going on and my voice shaking as I told him we were at the hospital. He asked me what the address was and I said I didn't know!

The nurse, Becky had started chest compressions and you were lying there, completely unconscious while she did the compressions. Then a girl dressed in scrubs came running out of the front door and I called to her, "What's the address?!" She ran toward us and told me and then I think nurse Becky yelled at her to bring the defibrillator. Honestly, it seemed like minutes before nurse Micaela came out with the defibrillator.

The dispatcher was asking me if there was an AED and I said that one was coming. They came out with it and then they shocked you. It made an awful sound (like electricity) and Becky started compressions again and nurse Vicki gave you mouth-to-mouth. I tried to hang up on the dispatcher and he said that he had to stay on the line till someone got there.

The fire truck arrived first and I guess they took over. I told the dispatcher good-bye and just stood there, staring at what was going on. I guess you were revived at that point. I recall someone saying, "He's back." They called your name and I leaned over and said your name too. Your eyes just kind of rolled back in your head.

The EMT guys came too around this time and brought a board to put under you. They rolled you to your side and slid it under you. Then they put you in the ambulance and took off. I just kind of stood there in shock. Becky hugged me, and I started to cry. We all talked for a few minutes and then I got in my car and called Thomas and Betty.

I drove to the ER and there was Betty and Robert! Robert had cut his hand and was there just by coincidence. I was worried that your mother needed to know, so I called Thomas and he drove by her house, but no one came to the door. I guess I called Ashley because she came around this time.

The chaplain came out and asked if there was anything he could do. So of course I asked him to pray for you and we all just leaned in as he asked for your protection and God's love to surround you. After the prayer, I asked him if he could get your phone. We looked for a number for your mother but I couldn't find it, and then it occurred to me to look for Harold's number.

A while later, the ER doc came out and said you were stable and that one person could go back for a minute to see you. I went and you were lying there as still as could be. I said your name and you opened your eyes and said, "Hi, Mom." Then you closed them and wouldn't really open them again. I prayed for you and held your hand and then had to leave.

I guess that's how I remember things. I hope this helps!!!

BETHESDA HEALTH CLINIC NURSES' EYEWITNESS ACCOUNT

Bethesda nurse, Rebecca Hernandez, tells the story in first person from her point of view.

I had arrived at work between 7:45 and 7:55 AM. I started walking toward the clinic and a lady parked at the clinic asked if I were a nurse. I said, "Yes." She said that her friend was sick. As I walked around the front of the car, she then said, "And, I think he is not breathing." As I got close to the passenger door, her friend was slumped back between the seats; his neck was hanging back and his eyes were open and set. As I began checking him out, I gave my phone to the lady to call 911. I checked for a pulse and learned that he didn't have one. I think what the lady said was, "He was sick, not injured." I grabbed him by his T-shirt and pulled him out of the car—at least I got half his body out. He was pretty long, and I only needed his upper body on the ground. I rechecked his pulse once I got him on the ground. He still didn't have a pulse. So, I started chest compressions. The lady was on the phone talking to 911. They were trying to locate where Bethesda Clinic was by address and phone number.

I had started my second set of compressions when Micaela came out to ask if I needed help. I asked her to bring the defibrillator and ambulance bag and get help. While I was doing compressions, Vicki, another

Bethesda nurse, got there and started CPR on him. As we were working on the young man, Amanda, a Bethesda doctor, came with the AED. I continued compressions while Vicki was applying the pads from the AED. Once the pads were applied, the machine recommended that a shock be given. As we cleared away from the young man, the button was pressed for a shock to be administered. He was shocked, but he didn't come back after the first shock. The machine instructions read "continue with compressions." Becky resumed with compression. The fire department arrived shortly after the second compressions were administered. At that time, we changed positions. One fireman took over compressions and another fireman took over respirations. The ambulance arrived after the fire department, and they continued working on him. The young man then started breathing!!

THOMAS EYEWITNESS ACCOUNT

Thomas tells this part of the story in first person.

After the ETMC ambulance took you to the hospital on Beckham Street, I saw you for a few minutes, and then Betty and Ashley went back separately to see you too. After they saw you, I went and sat with you while arrangements were being made to take you over to Cardiac ICU. You were very still and seemed to be asleep. A nurse came in to give you a shot of something and that woke you up. You started shivering and couldn't stop, so I asked for a blanket. The nurse brought a warm one, and once she covered you up, you stopped shivering and went back to sleep.

Thomas came and talked to you, and you said, "Hi, Brother Lawrence." Then you went back to sleep. Thomas sat with you, and since it was lunch time, Ashley and I went to the cafeteria and ate. Thomas called and said that they were moving you to ICU, so we went there where they had you in a cubicle. You were talking and asking what had happened. Thomas, Ashley, and I were there. You asked many times what had happened and seemed worried that a woman had put something in your water on Sunday night that might have caused everything. You were very groggy.

After a while, I left to go home for a few minutes, and Ashley stayed with you. Thomas went back to PATH. I think that's when your Mama and Harold came. I got back shortly after that, and then they asked all the visitors to leave from 2:00 to 4:00. We went and sat in the waiting room and visited for a while. Then William, Larry, and James came to see you. They let each one of them in separately for just a few minutes.

I left to go eat, and when I got back, your mom was still there. We visited for a while, and then John, Shane, and Jerald showed up. Alice came a little later, and we all held hands and each one of us prayed for you.

MY EYEWITNESS ACCOUNT OF DAYS THAT FOLLOWED

Here the narration becomes mine:

Friday: I left ICU on Friday evening and moved to a private room. I received many visits from my church family.

Saturday: On Saturday I also had many visitors. Thomas and his wife, Mom Deborah; Betty and her husband, Tim; Jerald and his wife, Sherry, son, Jason, and granddaughter, Mindy; Shane; John; my brother, Malone and his girlfriend, Teresa, from Dallas; also from Dallas, my friend, Clarence. Alice and her son, Garrett, visited too.

Sunday: Glenwood brought church to me. We had church in a secluded area in the hospital. We took communion and had a good church service. I can't remember all who came from Glenwood that particular day, but I know it was the members of Glenwood Church of Christ. My church prayed for me, and I prayed for myself. I prayed for God's will to be done. They encouraged me and hugged me. I received visits all day Sunday. I also struggled mentally Sunday because I did not want to have the surgery. I didn't want to have the ICD (Implantable Cardiac Defibrillator) put in my chest. There was definitely a spiritual struggle within my mind and my body. Many people encouraged me to get the ICD, yet I hadn't decided to do so. I went to bed Sunday night still undecided. The doctors and nurses instructed me not to eat or drink anything after midnight.

Monday: After praying, peace finally came to my spirit. I had decided to allow them to implant the ICD in my chest. I began to receive visits Monday morning. People continued to ask me what was my decision, and I began telling them that I changed my mind. People began to thank me for deciding to take what Jesus had provided for me. There was so much pressure on me on Monday, it was overwhelming.

They had scheduled me for surgery at 5:00 PM. I was expecting them to come get me at 5:00, but I was surprised when they came in around 4:10 PM and asked me, "Are you ready?" I said, "I thought you were coming at 5:00 PM." They said, "That's the time your surgery is scheduled. We have to make preparations for the surgery." I said, "Okay, then." I told my Mama bye and that I loved her. She said she loved me too. They took me off the bed and laid me flat on a bed with wheels and strapped me down. They began rolling me to the room where they were going to perform surgery on me. When we got there, they first had me sign all the papers concerning the surgery. I read them quickly and signed them. Next, they started putting all the tubes in me, and I saw the lady get that long needle to put me to sleep. So, I turned my head the opposite direction. I don't like to watch those needles go into my body. Next, I began to fall asleep. I was knocked out by the time Dr. Sam arrived.

They put in the ICD and returned me to my room. My mother was still there when I returned. They transferred me back to the bed in my room.

They gave me a handful of paperwork with instructions. I read them and ate. I chatted with my Mama for a few hours. I think Mama Deborah came back to check on me. She stayed briefly and left. My mother left late that night. I went to sleep.

<u>Tuesday</u>: I awoke Tuesday morning sore, but I felt peaceful. My mother showed up early. Then Renea came to check on me. She visited briefly, hugged me and left. I watched TV and chatted with my mama until Mom Deborah showed up around dinner time. She was trying to persuade me to leave before they brought me dinner. I asked her to allow me to eat my very last meal there, so she did. I said, "Thanks, Mom, for waiting and understanding that I was hungry." I ate and started gathering all my belongings, getting ready to depart. My sister-in-law, Stacy, came in for a minute. She chatted with my mother and me briefly, then she took my mother home.

Shortly after they left, Mom Deborah took me to her house. I brushed my teeth, used the restroom, and went to sleep. During the morning hours, the Lord Jesus sent me a vision. In the vision, I saw Mom Deborah tending me as a nurse. I knew then for certain everything was proceeding accordingly as Jesus Christ had planned it.

Wednesday: Wednesday morning I woke and brushed my teeth. Mom Deborah and I ate breakfast together at her house. I told her about the vision, and she was pleased at hearing it.

Today (11/4/2013): Today I'm taking meclizine medication for vertigo (motion sickness) that began Monday evening after my surgery. My heart is fine now with the ICD. So far, I haven't had any problems with it. I have been able to run and to walk, but I'm timid about running due to my heart condition. Time will change that. I don't feel normal, but I look normal.

Currently, I go to different churches, testifying about my physical death and resurrection. The Lord Jesus Christ has commissioned me to do so. I will testify wherever I am as long as the Holy Spirit is leading me to do so. Though this commission is not easy, I must go in His name by His authority, testifying of His power and glory.

The Lord says, "Don't persuade nor convince the people but rather just testify of My works." So, I just testify, like He says. So far, I have gone to two churches and shared my testimony, and they both received me with gladness and believed the Holy Spirit had sent me to testify of His works. I testified at The Gathering at The Benevolence Center in downtown Tyler, TX, Under the Bridge Ministry and also at Glenwood Church of Christ, where I am a member.

Chapter 2

TESTIMONY OF A THANKFUL PATIENT

Lawrence Hodges died in the Bethesda Health Clinic parking lot.

Gang violence, drugs, and prison were a part of Lawrence's life for many years. But in 2006, while serving a life sentence in prison, Lawrence became a Christian. He studied with the prison ministry, and lived in the 'faith-based' wing, and trained for eighteen months to become a ministry facilitator.

"God told me I would be free one day, and I believed Him," said Lawrence, and he was granted parole after serving nineteen years. However, with his record, no one would rent him an apartment, and no one would give him a job. "I was just trying to survive," said Lawrence, "some days just trying to eat!"

Bethesda volunteer, Betty and her friend, Deborah, whom Lawrence now calls his "godmothers," came into his life through a ministry of Glenwood Church of Christ. They helped him search for a job and housing, prayed with him, went to church with him, and encouraged and lifted him up in every way they could. With their help, Lawrence found a couple of part-time jobs, an apartment, and started building a life and attending truck driving school.

Lawrence became a Bethesda patient because his jobs didn't offer health insurance. Bethesda Health Care is a clinic that provides medical care to those in need. And he found more than health care at Bethesda. "The Scriptures on the walls tell you that these people are believers," said Lawrence. "They take care of people here, and they believe in Jesus."

After Lawrence fainted two days in a row for no apparent reason, he visited Deborah's to get her advice. Deborah took one look at Lawrence and said, "Let's go to Bethesda!"

On the short drive from Deborah's home to Bethesda, Lawrence fainted again... and stopped breathing. "I looked over at him, and I just knew he was gone," said Deborah.

Going as fast as she could, Deborah careened into the Bethesda parking lot, where medical staff member Becky Hernandez had just arrived. Immediately, Becky pulled Lawrence from the car and started CPR.

From inside the clinic, Micaela Cintron noticed what was happening and summoned nurse Vicki Garcia and nurse practitioner Amanda Rosales, who brought out the defibrillator. They shocked Lawrence twice before the ambulance and EMTs arrived and shocked him again. "He's back," said the paramedic when Lawrence finally started breathing.

In the ETMC Emergency Room, Dr. Brad King was on duty. As the husband of Dr. Kendra King, who had been a part of Bethesda staff from the beginning, he was very familiar with Bethesda's ministry. Lawrence was diagnosed with Brugada Syndrome, a genetic disease that causes a lethal arrhythmia in the heart. Within weeks, a defibrillator and pacemaker were installed in his heart.

"God used Bethesda Health Clinic in a powerful way," asserts Deborah Smith. "Why did I drive to Bethesda that morning instead of the emergency room? Why was everyone 'on point' and able to help Lawrence right away?"

Lawrence knows the answers. "When God is in the plan, you can't mess up the plan," he said.

Following his diagnosis, Lawrence understood the importance of working on his overall physical health. He attended nutrition classes at Bethesda, and learned about healthy eating and how to cook healthy meals.

Since then, Lawrence has returned to prison, but not as a prisoner... as a part of a prison ministry team!

Bethesda Health Clinic
409 West Ferguson Street
Tyler, TX 75702
(903) 596-8353 main office number

"Validation of my physical death"

Herein are the facts of my physical death.

Facts:

#1 - No heartbeat for fifteen minutes

#2 - No pulse for fifteen minutes

#3 - I was shocked by a defibrillator twice. The first time they shocked me, there was no response in my body to the shock. So they had to re-set the defibrillator again for the second attempt to shock my heart back to a heartbeat. Okay!!! I'm about to challenge the born again Christians, followers of Jesus Christ but not the world, not the sinners. The Bible says clearly: The Holy Spirit will lead us and guide us in all truth (John 16:13). See, the believers have something that the world, sinners don't have, and that is the anointing of the Holy Ghost (1 John 2:27). The Apostle John says, But the anointing which you have received of him abides in you, and you need not any man teach you: but as the same anointing teaches you of all things, and is truth, and is no lie, and even as it hath taught you, you shall abide in him (1 John 2:27). I like the way the Apostle Paul said it in Romans 3:4—Let God be truth, but every man a lie (a liar)! Watch what the Lord Jesus Christ says in this passage in John.

John 20:29—Blessed are they that have not seen, and yet have believed. Jesus Christ rebuked doubting Thomas for his lack of faith. This portion of the book was written that the body of Christ, the saints of God, the followers of Jesus Christ, might believe the power of Jesus Christ's name and the power of the Holy Ghost. So glory, honor and praise to Jesus Christ, my personal Lord and Savior. There is no other name under Heaven among man by which we can be saved, except the name Jesus (Acts 4:12). Jesus Christ says, "I am the way, the truth and the life, and no man comes unto the Father except through me," (John 14:6). Amen! Amen! Amen!

Chapter 3

SPIRITUAL WARFARE

Before I decided to permit my surgeon, Dr. John Sam to implant an ICD in my chest, there were many negative thoughts racing through my head, saying: Don't have the surgery; it's not the Lord's will for your life. It could not be God's will. God would never permit you to do such a thing like that! God leads everyone divinely, or by way of medicine.

But not through a device. A device is never God's provision. I wrestled all day Sunday with the decision to allow them to implant this medical device in my chest and connect it with my heart. This decision was overwhelming for me. I prayed, and prayed and prayed, until finally, I got my peace about it and rest in my spirit. The Lord Jesus Christ gave me peace that this was His will for my life. So I eventually obeyed the Lord Jesus Christ by allowing the surgeons to implant this medical device in my heart. Something of such magnitude was too much for me to imagine, especially for my heart. You see, when and if people get something of this magnitude performed on their hearts, they need to be assured that God is in the plan. That way whatever happens, they will be right in the center of God's will and plan for their lives. We don't want to miss the Lord's plan, especially dealing with the human heart. The human heart is what keeps everything working, so no one wants to make the wrong decision with the human heart. Prayer is especially crucial for any decisions dealing with the heart. I think being certain of God's will for my life was more important to me than the surgery itself. The fear of surgery was not my greatest fear, but rather being outside the will of God by making the wrong decision about the surgery. Whether or not to have the surgery was my biggest problem.

I needed to be certain. I needed God's wisdom at that time as to what to do or not to do. It was a very, very tough time for me, in addition to the pressure from whether or not to have the surgery. Everyone was in my ear, praying and saying, "It's the Lord's will for you to have the surgery." I didn't believe then, though, because humans can be worldly and selfish when it comes to making medical decisions. So I had to get my peace from the Lord Jesus Christ myself.

I think and believe Christians don't mind dying, as long as they're certain to be in the Lord's will when He calls them home. I think there is a peace about death when you're certain to be right in the center of God's will for your life. That is so imperative and relevant to me, because we understand the message of the cross. Death is appointed unto man once to die, then, eternal life must follow. From a Christian's point of view or perspective, believers shall suffer for the name of Jesus Christ and some are willing to die for the sake of the gospel. Amen.

Chapter 4

PHYSICAL AND EMOTIONAL STRUGGLES WITH BPPV

Before, during, and after my experience with Brugada Syndrome, I suffered with "Benign Paroxysmal Positional Vertigo." This is a disorder arising in the inner ear. Its symptoms are repeated episodes of positional vertigo, which is a spinning sensation caused by changes in the position of the head. BPPV is the most common cause of the symptoms of vertigo.

On September 24, 2013, and September 26, 2013, I passed out. The first time I fell on my futon couch in my room at my place, and the second time I fell in the parking lot at my place. The entire time I was at ETMC, I was experiencing vertigo attacks. People had to assist me getting out of the bed at the hospital.

I was physically affected very much by BPPV. I had sleepless nights. I couldn't look directly up or down, because doing so would trigger an attack. I attempted to do the BPPV cure exercises, but it only got worse. I was affected by walking too fast or turning suddenly. I feared falling out of my bed due to an attack. My sleep would be taken away from me. Sometimes I would be afraid to attempt to go back to sleep again. If I tried to rest or sleep on my left side and/or my back, I would get an attack of vertigo. I couldn't look directly upward or downward. It would affect the vertigo. I could not tie my shoes while standing up straight.

I was prescribed a dizziness medication by the name of Meclazine. It only suppressed the vertigo—it didn't make it go away. So, I stopped taking it. It was only making me drowsy and sleepy. Secondly, I stopped doing the bed exercise too, because it only made my vertigo worse. Next, I started Googling about natural cures for vertigo and found the recommendation of using water, magnesium pills, and calcium as a cure. Mom Deborah didn't think I should adhere to the Internet sites because of many lies and falsehoods found there. So, we Googled another site, and it also spoke in favor of using a magnesium supplement to cure vertigo. So she said, "Go ahead and try it, but be careful."

I'm not very good at numbers so Mom Deborah used her phone and a pencil and paper to do the correct calculation for the proper water intake needed each day. I should drink one gallon of water daily along with

420 mg of magnesium and 1,000 mg of calcium per day. So, I took an old gallon milk jug and used it to make sure I got a gallon of water each day. I already had a brand new bottle of magnesium pills, which I had purchased almost five months before my physical death. The reason that I had already purchased the magnesium prior to the Brugada event was that I was trying to find anything to assist in healing my left wrist. I had also bought calcium pills in the past. I was wondering why I never threw the calcium and magnesium pills away, nor used them in the past. I just had the bottles in my closet in a bag. I was afraid to take them at that time. So, I just kept them stored in my closet for no apparent reason whatsoever. It's amazing how you can buy things out of ignorance and later use them for an unpredictable purpose.

I had great fear due to having BPPV "vertigo." I was depressed, afraid, anxious, doubtful, disappointed, lost and confused. I was overwhelmed with negative feelings.

Some people were telling me that the vertigo would go away, and some would tell me the very opposite. I didn't truly know what to believe. I was assigned to Dr. Crawford here in Tyler, TX, at the Bethesda Health Clinic. He continued to encourage me that he thought my vertigo would leave. When it seemed to be getting worse, Dr. Crawford said at that time, "Well, some people's bodies that have been through what yours has might not get everything back." Even though Dr. Crawford had said these things to me, deep inside my heart I believed one day God would heal me of the disorder, but I had no evidence to prove it in my body. I was basing my faith on the facts of the past, when I originally had vertigo three years ago while I was in prison. I guess, knowing that I was healed of it the first time gave me hope for my deliverance the second time. I just continued to pray and ask everyone else for prayer. I continued to drink one gallon of water daily and take my magnesium and calcium pills.

I would pray persistently, and I heard the Lord say one day, "It too shall pass." I know the Lord meant my vertigo would pass. After hearing the "good news" from the Lord Himself, I had peace. I kept praying and drinking all the water and taking the magnesium and calcium daily. Then, at or around December 8, 2013, the Lord revealed to me that He had already healed my vertigo. A few days after the Lord spoke that to me, the BPPV vertigo was cured. I slept on my left side and my back with no problem. I just remained in faith about it in silence, but NO MORE ATTACKS!

I called Bro. Thomas and asked him if I could bring the message the following Sunday after the Lord cured me of BPPV. He said that would be fine. I preached a message on Mark 5:1-34, and I related it to my deliverance from the vertigo disorder. I shared my story for the glory of Jesus Christ.

Date of message: December 16, 2013, "My Deliverance from Vertigo"

My Remedy for Vertigo

A. Prayer (James 5:16)

B. One gallon of water every single day until my deliverance came

C. 420 mg of magnesium

D. 1,000 mg of calcium

Chapter 5

MY BEGINNING

I, Lawrence Earl Hodges, was born on July 3, 1969 in Palestine, TX. Both of my parents were unsaved. They neither attended church nor took me to church. Church was not a common practice in my household as a child. Both of my parents were alcoholics. Often times I would see my parents drinking alcohol and arguing with each other. They would even fight at times after arguing and drinking. I was afraid as a child, watching my parents fight and argue often. I just wanted them to stop and get along with each other. Well, the fighting never ceased, neither did the drinking of alcohol. There was always confusion and chaos in our household. My father was always cursing at my mother or at one of the children.

As a child, I wanted to say something to my parents for fussing, fighting, and drinking, but I didn't want a spanking for intruding in grown folk business. My father raised me not to get into grown folk conversation unless I was invited into it, otherwise, I would get a spanking for it. Grown-ups and children didn't have verbal interaction much. If you were a child, then you just did whatever the adult says and say: "Yes sir," or "No sir," and "Yes ma'am," or "No ma'am." Those were the rules for adult and child verbal association. Kids were always wrong and my parents were always correct in any given situation.

My father never allowed me to interrupt. He said it was bad manners. We had to wash our hands before we ate any food and we couldn't put our elbows on the table. He said that was bad manners as well. When I was a child, my father used to take me to get my hair cut very low, it was called an Ivory League haircut. My father would get my hair cut at Queen St. on Border St. in Tyler, TX. A lady barber by the name of Odelle used to cut my hair every Friday evening after my father got off work from the City of Tyler. I would cry because I didn't want a haircut. I didn't like my hair to be cut low, so I would cry almost every time she cut my hair. Crying didn't do much good, because I still got the haircut, and on top of that my father made me stop crying and go to the bathroom to wash my face and said, "When you return; your face better be straight or else you will get a whipping at home." So, I washed my face and I came out of the bathroom with a straight countenance. When my father spoke of a whipping, he didn't play around. He meant business! So, I responded favorably.

My Beginning

My father didn't mind whipping me when I was wrong about a matter. My mother didn't whip me much; she mostly just gave the orders and my father did the whipping. My father would always tell my mother, "Just tell me when I come from work and I will deal with him." And Daddy wasn't playing about it. When we did wrong, we would be hoping our mother would forget or just forgive us for it. Sometimes we would even attempt to go to sleep, hoping that would work. And sometimes it would work. Our mama would say, "That boy did this or that but he's asleep now. So let him sleep for tonight or get him tomorrow." Mama would say, "I don't want to hear all that racket tonight."

When Daddy whipped us, we screamed. It was painful. My father most of the time showed us mercy at my mother's request. He honored her word when it came to discipline at times. Our father didn't believe in giving us many chances when we disobeyed our parents. His only recourse was a whipping.

As a boy, a child, a teenager, my father taught me how to clean bathrooms at a very young age. Cleaning the bathroom was my very first chore indoors, to commit to do twice a week. Yeah, I had to clean the bathroom on Monday and Thursday every week. As a teenager, my second indoors chore was washing dishes. My father said, "Now that you have learned how to clean the bathroom, I will teach you how to wash dishes." So, I learned how to wash dishes.

When I was a teenager, on Saturdays my father taught me how to do landscaping work. Before we would go over to our friend's house or even to the park, Daddy would say, "You all get the yard cleaned first, and after I examine it, you may leave for your friend's house." As boys, we also had a curfew. My father explained to me what a curfew meant. Then he would say, "You need to be home around or at dark or at 6:30 pm or 7:00 pm." The older I got, the later my father would grant my curfew.

My father and mother would always tell me to be careful crossing the streets. It would be easy for a child to get hit by a car, so caution was necessary crossing the streets. My parents would say, "Make sure it's clear both ways before you cross the street."

I think, the earliest as I can remember, I started hanging out with my best friend by the name of Kevin Nelson. He was my childhood friend from the fifth grade. I would go to his house and play with his toys and we would go across the street to play basketball. He lived directly across the street from T.J. Preston, the elementary school that we both went to as children, and where we met as friends. Kevin and I would play together until we got tired or until it got late, or until his mother would say, "Okay, boys, it's enough playing for today." Then we would say, "Yes, ma'am," to his mother. We would say a few words to one another and then I would go home.

My Beginning

When I was a child, my father very seldom allowed us to have company at our house. He persuaded us to go to our friends' houses to play and hang with them at their houses. Sending his children to their houses was his relief and way of getting peace and quiet, because we had a large family and there was always noise at our house.

When I was a young boy, my father taught me how to gamble. Yes, he taught me how to shoot or roll dice for pennies. Shooting dice became a common practice in our household for a pastime event. My father eventually increased the amount from pennies to nickels, dimes and quarters, etc. We eventually were betting a dollar bill against one another shooting dice. Eventually, I stole a pair of dice from my father and started shooting dice away from my house with my friends. We would shoot dice at my friends' houses or at the ball park in an alley, or anywhere we could roll the dice, basically.

Next, my father taught me how to play cards. He taught me how to play several card games. I eventually took the card game to the streets to use it to gamble and make money to survive. Finally, my father taught me how to shoot pool. I learned how to shoot pool and became good in time. I then started gambling at it for money. I would gamble against people in the neighborhood shooting pool. Gambling at a very young age became my life and survival means. I kept extra money in my pocket by playing either one of these pastimes.

Chapter 6

TAKING AND BREAKING

At the age of thirteen, I can clearly remember hanging out with an older friend by the name of Clint Smith. His family had just moved to Tyler, TX. He and I made friends at Peter Claver ball park. We played baseball and basketball at Peter Claver park. My family and I stayed directly across the street from a park in our neighborhood. Clint and I would play basketball together. After becoming friends, Clint influenced me to break into "old" houses with him. We were only breaking into old houses and "old" cars. We were looking for old coins. There was a rumor about certain old coins that could make one rich, so Clint and I were only looking for old coins. Especially for a wheat penny with 43 P on the back of it. So, I started a collection of old coins shortly after my search for old and antique coins. I started to save and hunt for old coins. Wherever I could look for old coins, I would. I just thought one day I would find the right old coin to become rich. Some old coins seemed to be valuable and antique.

For a course of two years, Clint and I were friends and we continued to break into abandoned houses and old cars for old coins and antique coins. Since we couldn't find the (1943 P) wheat penny, we decided to start a collection of old coins altogether. Perhaps one day something would come of it. After quite some time Clint and I seemed to part for no good reasons. We just sort of started fading away from each other. One day I realized he had moved on with his life and I needed to find another friend.

During my teenage years, I started to take things that didn't belong to me. If I didn't have money for what I wanted, I would go to the stores and just put it in my pocket and leave. I didn't really care whether or not I was caught for stealing. I just wanted things that I didn't have money for, so I stole to own it or have it. It was just a way of life for a teenager from the north side of Tyler, TX, in that era. I came up in the early 80s and it was hard on us coming up without much. We were poor and so we stole to have things that our parents were not able to afford. We had a family of eight siblings total. A large family. We didn't receive allowances as some children did for making good grades in school, or for being obedient at home. So, we learned how to take from stores. We would steal anything to make a dollar to have money in our pocket. We stole from everywhere we could steal from. We stole from drug stores, department and convenience stores.

I will never forget one day when we were stealing money from a car wash that was on Bow St. Our stealing finally came to a halt. We had crow bars and we were vandalizing the machines for coins. Well, one morning while we were sneaking into the car wash for coins, someone called the police on us. We all took off as we saw the police coming. I ran and tried to slide under a car but I was caught before I could get under it. The police arrested me first. They asked me about the other people, and I didn't tell them anything, but they caught them anyways. My oldest brother, Harry, was apprehended next, and finally they apprehended my best friend and partner in crime, by the name of Lenny Dave Mathis. They caught all three of us in one hour. The police took me and my best friend to juvenile, because we were minors, but they took my oldest brother to jail, because he was seventeen years old at the time. My friend Lenny Mathis and I were only fifteen years old at the time of our first arrest.

I stayed in the juvenile detention center for a couple of months until school started back, then they let me out on probation for the car wash theft. The institution in which I was stationed was called Roberts, a juvenile detention center in Tyler, TX. My mother visited me in Roberts Detention Center, and she had to sign papers for my release. I told my mama that I wanted out of that place. I can still remember being all alone in that one room by myself for two months. The bed was hard as steel and I felt deprived of all my freedom and rights. After I was released from Roberts, I returned to school in time with my peers. Some of my friends heard about me going to the juvenile detention center and made fun of me at school. I was embarrassed about what had happened to me. I just kept quiet about everything and resumed stealing again.

I said to myself, I will leave alone the car wash and just steal from the stores, since I had never been caught stealing from the stores. So, I did. I used to steal soft drinks from the soft drink water plant. We would go under the gate and steal soft drinks and sell them. I stole cigarettes by the carton and sold them to the gas station for $5.00 a carton to keep money in my pocket. I used to pick up cans and sell them to a man down the street. Since the man didn't have a dog, we would steal the cans back from him and re-sell them to him in a different bag on a different day. I never took more than one bag on each unexpected visit, so he would not be able to tell that I was stealing his cans and re-selling them to him.

During my teenage years, as I mentioned before, my father taught me how to play pool, shoot dice, and play cards. Once I learned how to master these games, I started carrying a pair of dice in my pocket to shoot dice for money. Then I started to carry a deck of cards in my back pocket to play for money. I would go to the pool hall on Morris Street in North Tyler to gamble at pool. My stealing increased to support my gambling

Taking And Breaking

habit. I then realized that I was addicted to gambling. So, I started cheating for my gambling addiction. I started cutting my dice on the numbers (six or eight). My friends would have to give me a cut of half of the bet because they were my dice. Cutting the dice was common, if you owned a pair and everyone liked you. Everyone liked me in the neighborhood, so cutting was not a problem. Only one problem with cutting: you could not do both. You could either cut the dice or shoot the dice. I needed guaranteed money, so I cut the dice instead.

Moving along: I went to Dogan Middle School on Border Ave., on the north side of Tyler, TX, for all my middle school years. I failed the sixth grade when I first arrived in middle school. I had to repeat the sixth grade, and on my second time through I got promoted to the seventh grade. Then I had to take summer school my seventh grade year to be promoted to the eighth grade, due to lack of credits to be promoted to the eighth grade. When I finally got promoted, I was so happy. I couldn't believe I was finally in the eighth grade. I was growing up.

I struggled with my grades my eighth grade year. I guess after failing once already in the sixth grade, I had doubt that I could repeat the eighth grade again. I was hoping to pass through. I really wanted to move on with my peers. So, I studied more my eighth grade year and was hoping to be promoted with my classmates. Well, I can remember telling Coach Barns that I didn't want to have to repeat his class again next year. I can remember him telling me, "Do your best and you will pass okay." I really think Coach Barns had pity on me and gave me a break my eighth grade year.

Well, the school year was ending and no one really knew whether or not they passed, especially me. So, we awaited the report card in the mail. When they arrived, by the grace of God, I was promoted to the ninth grade. I was so happy! I was ready to go to John Tyler. Then, my father decided to move our family to the west side of Tyler, TX, by the neighborhood "White City." I was very upset about the move; because I wanted to be around my homeboys and all my peers from my childhood days.

So I had to go to Robert E. Lee high school for my freshman year. I didn't know anyone there, so I had to make new friends and start all over again in a new neighborhood. It was difficult for me. I didn't have anyone to hang out with. I was all alone. My first year in the west side, I had a fight with E. B. Jackson for making fun of my clothing. As soon as we got off the bus, I hit him in the mouth and busted his lip. I became scared after he saw the blood, because he was ready to fight. We put up our fists to fight and he struck me in the jaw. Then, everyone broke the fight up and encouraged us to let it go. So we stopped. The next day, we didn't speak. Then, shortly afterwards, E.B. Jackson and I became best friends in "White City." The fight that we had early on in our friendship brought us into a friendship. We played basketball together and we spent time together at his house in the neighborhood. I was at his house more than my own sometimes. It's funny how a fist fight brought us into a good friendship. We never had any more problems between us.

Next, I met another young man by the name of Brian Barton. He was one of my gambling partners too. Brian and I sold roses together for Mr. Day in Fort Worth, TX. We would ride all the way to Fort Worth to sell some Tyler Roses. We worked for Mr. Day for a while until one day we met an old man by the name of Mr. Belcher. He had his own landscaping business. Mr. Belcher hired both of us, me and Brian. We made pretty good money as young teenagers. Learning to do landscaping for money on the side was a good thing for me and Brian. It kept me out of trouble and kept me busy. Brian and I mostly worked on the weekends. I really enjoyed working for Mr. Belcher; he paid us every day after each work day. He paid us cash money. As soon as we got paid, we would gamble against each other, playing cards. I would go to Brian's house and to his front porch, or we would play in his bedroom. We would play until someone got broke. Then, the card game would end.

I met Ray Wilson next, at Pete Elementary School, playing basketball. Ray also went to Robert E. Lee with me. Ray and I became gambling buddies, playing cards against one another. We would have to play at his house because my father didn't allow me to gamble against my friends in our living quarters. He felt that was disrespecting our home. Only family and relatives could be privileged to do that. So, Ray and I gambled all over his house and outside. Ray's parents didn't care. As long as we weren't fighting and arguing, everything else was permissible.

I started gambling against my own siblings and parents. Yes, my parents would shoot dice against us as children. Our aunts and uncles would come over to gamble with us. We would all shoot dice against each other and play card games against each other. When I lost, sometimes I would steal the money back from my parents and from my siblings. I refused to be broke or to stay broke. I started gambling against my best friend, Lenny Mathis, my other friends, Brian Barton, Ray Wilson, and E. B. Jackson. If I didn't win honestly, then I would cheat to get more money to play again. Whatever I had to do to get my money back, I was willing to do it, as long as I didn't get caught cheating red-handed.

This was because if you got caught cheating red-handed, then it would ruin the gambling friendship. So I worked very hard not to get caught cheating while I was gambling in anything whatsoever.

I reunited with a friend from middle school by the name of Lenny Dave Mathis. His mother moved to "White City" next, so he and I started back hanging out together. This is when he and I began to really gamble against one another tough. I would go to his house and we would gamble for electronics if he didn't have any money. It didn't matter to me. We would agree to a price for the item and we would gamble for it. I would win most of the time. Then, I would have to find a way to carry the electronic item to my house. I did not care what it was, I wanted to win it if he had it. He and I spent long hours playing cards. I would take turns with all my friends and gamble with them.

I even met a boy from my high school my freshman year by the name of Kevin Foster. His parents owned a café, so we played pool for money. I had to ride my bicycle to St. Foris to gamble with him at pool. Kevin and I became pool table hustlers. That's all we would gamble on: pool.

My father left my mother in 1985 and he moved back to Houston, by himself. I lived in Tyler another year. Then, I wanted to leave Tyler, but I didn't know where to go. So, I asked my mama to ask my father about moving to Houston with him. My father said, "Okay, send him on the bus." My mother said: "Yes, you may go live with your father in Houston." I said, okay.

My mama bought me a bus ticket from Greyhound and I made an appointment for my departure. My mama took me to the bus station in her car. We got out of the car and went inside. She remained with me until my bus was ready to leave. She told me, "Call your father when you get to Houston, and he will pick you up, okay?" I said, "Yes, ma'am." My mother hugged me and kissed me. I got on the bus and we waved at one another until I left Tyler.

I went to sit in the back of the bus. I found a good seat, sat down by myself and enjoyed my ride. It was a very long ride for me. Considering I had never been away from home for a long period, anyways. As we were traveling to Houston, I had no idea what to think. I was leaving my hometown; that's all I knew. I had never been to Houston for any such reason and here I was moving to the largest city in Texas. I was sightseeing the entire ride. We finally got to Interstate 45 S. We rode on it for quite a while until we finally made it to downtown Houston. I asked someone on the bus, "How far are we from the bus station?" They said, "We should be there in a few minutes." I said, "Thanks a lot!" I pulled out my father's phone number to call him.

In a few more minutes, we arrived at the Greyhound bus station. I got off the bus and remembered to get my luggage from underneath the bus. That's where they stored extra luggage. I showed my ticket to the driver and received my extra luggage. I went inside the station and called my mother, first. I said, "Hey, Mama. I have just arrived here in Houston, finally. It was a long trip, Mama." She said, "Yeah, it's a long way from East Texas. Well, call your father and tell him to come and pick you up, okay? Enjoy your father and be a good boy." I said, "Yes, ma'am." She said, "Stay in touch with me, son. I love you!" I said, "I love you too, Mama." We both said goodbye and hung up the phone.

I called my father. He answered the phone. I said, "Daddy, I'm here at the bus station. Are you coming to pick me up?" He said, "Yeah, give me a minute

Taking And Breaking

and I will be there, okay?" I said, "Okay, Daddy." We both hung up the phone. In about twenty minutes, my father arrived to pick me up. I saw him and he pulled off the road so I could get in his car and put my luggage in. I put all my luggage in the car and we drove away. We got to my father's house. I took all my luggage in the house.

Then my father called me to sit down and talk with him. He said, "Son, you're in another city now. I'm going to lay down the law here in Houston with you. Either you can obey me here in Houston, or you can go back to Tyler, where you came from." I said, "Okay, Daddy. I will do what you say, Daddy. I won't give you any problems, Daddy." He said, okay.

My daddy said, "Come and let me show you your room." I said, "Okay, Daddy." He said, "This middle room will be yours." He showed me the entire room and said, "Make yourself at home." I unpacked all my luggage and got comfortable in my new residence. I went outside to see how the grass and outdoors looked there. I knew I would be doing the landscaping there too. So, I was preparing myself for it. My father raised me to do landscaping, so it was a must at home.

My father told me early on in my arrival stage that I was not the son that he and my mama had discussed coming to live with him, but my brother, Leroy instead. But he said, "Since you're already here, you may stay too." I said, "Okay, Daddy." So, he sent for my brother Leroy to come to Houston. In about two weeks after my arrival, here comes Leroy on the Greyhound bus. My daddy told me one day, "Let's go to the bus station to pick up your brother, Leroy." I said, "Fine." We got in the car and went to pick him up at the bus station. I assisted him with all his luggage and property. We put everything in the trunk of my father's car and we drove away. When we arrived home, my daddy told my brother, Leroy to put everything down in the front room and come to the bedroom. He told my brother the same thing that he told me. "You will obey me here in Houston, or you may take your bags and go back to Tyler. Do we have that understood?" My brother replied by saying, "Yes sir, Daddy." Daddy said, "Okay. Go ahead and take your bags in the room where your brother sleeps. You all will have the same room, okay?" Leroy said, "Okay, Daddy." Leroy came in the room with me and I showed him around in our new room. He had his own bed and I had my own, but we shared the same dresser drawers and closet.

Everything was new for both of us. We were in a new city with our father. We did not have any friends. School had not started yet. My father got us both enrolled into school. I went to Wortham High School on Reed Rd., and my brother, Leroy went to middle school on Belfort Blvd. After school we started making friends in the neighborhood. Things started to unfold and we both had new challenges ahead of us. We met some people three houses from the left of where we lived. They had a basketball goal. We asked them if they minded that we played basketball at their house sometimes. They said, "No problem. Just respect our goal and balls and come at a decent hour." We both agreed to do so. So, we started playing basketball at their house all the time.

We became friends with all our neighbors. Everyone seemed to like both of us. Life was starting to seem different. I had new friends. I wasn't stealing anymore from stores, and I finally got to meet my four older brothers in Houston from my Dad's previous marriage. My father had told us about them, yet we had never met them in person. We met them and we became family and had fellowship afterwards. Our older brothers got us involved with church. They would come pick us up and take us to church with them. They had a flag football team and they taught us to play it with them. We had a lot of fun playing flag football with our older brothers.

I must say that I finally started doing my homework. My grades changed dramatically. I went from making F's on my report card to making B's and C's. I thought this was unheard of. I would never have dreamed of this in a million years! This was because I wanted to be a "drop out" just last year. Well, I knew my older brothers wouldn't go for me failing, and besides, I wanted a better life; but didn't know how to get it. I just didn't have any hope whatsoever! I mean, mine!

My life was starting to shift somewhat. I couldn't steal anymore from stores. I had put all my gambling habits on hold, because life was different in Houston.

Besides, I didn't have those bad influences anymore. So, I just went to school and spent time with my family there in Houston. This was also a time to get to know my other brothers and bond with them, since we didn't grow up together. This was a great opportunity to get familiar with one another.

Well, the school year went well. I made good grades and I got promoted to the eleventh grade. When school was out, my father met a guy at the cafe down the street. The guy started treating my Dad with free alcohol drinks. Well, my father, like most people, didn't turn down those free drinks. Those free drinks turned into a visit on our front porch to read his newspapers, daily. Well, as you may know, he had a hidden motive for buying my father free drinks and he started calling my daddy "Pops." Well, I was a teenager at the time, so I couldn't figure out what his intentions were. Things still seemed strange to me, even then. I couldn't say anything, because it was grown people's business and I was still considered living in my father's house. So I had to keep quiet about his business.

Anyway, the man started buying us food and gradually hanging around our house more frequently. The man slowly started coming inside our father's house to use the restroom and sit around inside. We learned later this man was a well-known drug dealer in Houston. I think by the time Daddy realized it, it was already too late to distance himself from him. He chose not to tell the man to take his stuff and leave. The man started inviting his other drug friends and his workers to my

Taking And Breaking

father's house. It's like they were trying to take over my father's house, slowly. The man was watching his drug houses across the street from my father's house.

When we realized what this man was doing, it was shocking and scary. It was terrible. The drug dealer had me holding all his jewelry for him. He would pay me to watch his jewelry for him. Our home was no longer a safe refuge. We no longer knew what might happen at my father's house. Everyone was afraid at this house from this point forward. My brother, Leroy got a bus ticket and went back to Tyler. My father was no longer staying at the house. I mean, he would come over to pay the bills and leave. Our father's house was now unsafe for living. I was the only one there at times, not knowing what to do.

Then, one day, an unexpected visitor came to visit our house. It was the Houston Police Department. When the police officer knocked on the back door, I peeped out the window at first. Then, I thought, "We're all in trouble." I went to the back door after delaying in answering it. I said, "Hello." The policeman responded, "Is the guardian here?" I said, "No sir." He said, "Well, tell your father we (the police) need to have a talk with him." I said, "Yes sir! Will do." The policeman left afterwards.

I called my Aunt Jill's house. I knew where my father was located. I ask my Aunt Jill to put my father on the phone. He got on the phone. I said, "Daddy, the police came by your house today looking for you. They want to talk with you." He asked, "About what?" I said, "They didn't say, but you can speculate as to why, Daddy. The traffic at our house with the drug dealer and all his friends. That's probably why, Daddy." He said, "Probably so." I said, "Well, are you coming home, Daddy?" He replied, "Later." I said, "Okay, Daddy." I remained living there for a week or so alone. Then I gave the drug dealer all his jewelry back. He asked me why I was giving him all his jewelry back. I said, "Because I'm going back to Tyler, where I came from. This is not the life I want to live."

The drug dealer offered me a job to drive for him, but I turned it down. I took all the money that I had made from the drug dealer and called myself a cab to go back to Tyler. I got all my clothes together, and by the time the cab arrived at my door, I was ready to go. I called my father back and told him that I had called a cab to take me to the Greyhound bus station. "Well, Daddy, I love you. Sorry things had to end this way. But I didn't want this drug dealer to get me in trouble with the police. I love you, Daddy. I will call you and let you know when I arrive in Tyler again." I got to the bus station, I paid the cab driver his fare, and I asked when the next bus left for Tyler. The people told me, so I waited patiently until my time was ready.

When I heard them call for my bus, I got up and grabbed all my luggage and went to put it under the bus, then I went to sit down on the bus. I asked the bus driver to make sure my bus was headed to Tyler. The bus driver said, "Yes. This bus is going to Tyler." I said, "Thank you, sir." I sat down afterwards. After sitting down, I started thinking about my father and his house. All I could think was that this could not be true, but it was in fact true. I got run out of my father's house by a known drug dealer in Houston, Texas. I was thankful to God that my brother, Leroy left a week before me.

There were so many thoughts in my head while I was riding back to Tyler. I was so thankful to God for not allowing either my brother or me to get into trouble with this whole ordeal. Finally, I got to Tyler. I called my father and told him that I made it back home safely. I had a good trip! I told my father that I loved him; and that I hoped he could overcome this situation at his house. My father said, "Yes, I will take care of it, son, thanks!" I told my father goodbye, and he said, "Okay, son." I then called my mother and asked her to come pick me up at the bus station. She said, "Okay, son. Give me a minute and I will be there." I said, "Okay, Mama." We both hung up the phone. In a while, my mother drove up and I was already standing outside, waiting on her. She got out of the car and assisted me with my bags. I got in the car and we took off. We arrived at her house. I saw all my siblings at the door. They came and hugged me and assisted me with all my bags. I went inside their house.

They had moved in a year. They were on S. Confederate when I left Tyler, but by the time I came back, they had moved to Old Noonday Rd., a few blocks down the street. After getting all my luggage inside the house, I sat down and chatted with my family. I asked my mother to call my Aunt Denise in Dallas, to see whether or not she would let me stay with her and her children until I graduated from high school. My mother called my Aunt Denise and surprisingly she said, yes, but provided that I obeyed her rules at home: kept good grades in and got along with her two daughters, Susan and Karen. I said, "Yes, ma'am. I will do all that you ask me to do, Aunt Denise." She told my mama to tell me to catch the bus to Dallas, and she would pick me up at the Greyhound bus station. I said, "Yes ma'am." My mother and I hung up the phone with my Aunt Denise. My mother and I found out which bus trip was best for me to take.

My mother took me to the bus station. I hugged my mother and kissed her and she sent me on my way to Dallas. I got to Dallas, and my Aunt Denise came to the bus station to pick me up. I got all my luggage and put it in her car. Aunt Denise turned off the radio and started telling me all that she expected of me as her nephew. I said, "Yes ma'am." We made it to her house and I saw both of her daughters, Susan and Karen. I hugged them both and kissed them. My aunt had a futon couch. She told me to sleep on the futon couch and said, "This is your bedroom." The living room was my bedroom and the guest closet was where I kept all my property. I didn't complain. I was thankful and glad she took me in as a tenant-guest.

I immediately started putting in applications for jobs. My two cousins both worked at Taco Bell on Marsh Lane and Forest Lane. I put in an application for Taco

Bell where my cousins were working. My cousin, Susan talked to her manager for me and they hired me the very same week that I moved to Dallas. This was my very first legal job. This was all new to me, working for money. I hadn't ever worked before, so I had no idea what it felt like to receive a check from an employer. It was pretty awesome to receive a check for working on a job. I was like, "I'm making real money for a change." This was not landscaping money nor money from gambling or hustling in the streets. It was a great feeling! I felt important for once in my life. I had never had this feeling before. I guess it was because I was working for a living and earning honest money. I didn't have to worry about anyone trying to take it from me.

I liked my first and new job as a cashier at Taco Bell. It felt good to work with and alongside of both of my girl cousins, Susan and Karen. We worked together and laughed together and rode home together in the same car. My cousin, Susan taught me how to use the city bus in Dallas, the DART Bus. She gave me a bus schedule and taught me how to ride the city bus. The city bus took me directly in front of my job on Forest Lane.

I met a young man at my job at Taco Bell by the name of C.B. Pruitt. C.B. and I became friends at work. School started shortly after C.B. and I became friends, so we started hanging out together. C.B. took me under his wing and taught me about Dallas little by little. Well, school was about to start and everyone was starting to go shopping for school clothes and supplies, so C.B. did so, too. We went to different department stores to school shop, like Marshalls, K-Mart, and to the mall. We shopped and bought our school clothes. C.B. also gave me some old clothes that he didn't want to wear the following school year. I accepted them and wore them too.

C.B. showed me around in our neighborhood. We would hang out together at the neighborhood park, Bachman Lake, which was a park and a lake. Everyone in the hood would hang out there on Sunday evenings especially.

School started in August and things were going well for me. I had a fresh start in the second largest city in Texas at the time (Dallas). I didn't know anyone on the first day of school except C.B. Pruitt. So, I just allowed him to show me around at the school for the first week, then I figured everything else out after that. I just went to class and home every day. I learned how to ride the school bus to school and back home. I rode the school bus with my cousin Karen. Susan went to Business Magnet her eleventh grade year. I was able to bond with my cousin Karen, since we rode the school bus together for school. Karen and I would chat coming and going to school sometimes. We would get home before Susan had to come from downtown, riding the city buses at times. Karen and I would start on our homework early.

Taking And Breaking

Both of my cousins were my motivations to be promoted to the next highest grade. I saw them doing their homework and working after school, so I thought, "I can do this too." There were no lazy people in the house, so I had to make passing grades too. So I did. I made decent grades and I didn't fail a single class. I must say, my best friend, C.B. was also a motivation for me being promoted to the next highest grade, and for working, because he was working too and he made good grades in school. I didn't have much room for slacking in work or school because my peers didn't do that.

Well, school had been going on and it was about to be Christmas time, so I planned to go visit my father for the Christmas holidays. I told my Aunt Denise of my plans for the Christmas holidays. I said, "Aunt Denise, I think I want to visit my father for the Christmas holidays." My Aunt Denise said, "Okay. son. Be safe and enjoy your visit. Tell your father hello for me." So I called my father and asked him whether or not I should visit him or not. My father said, "Yes. You may visit me for the Christmas holidays." I said, "Okay, Daddy. I will call you when I get to Houston, and you may pick me up at the Greyhound bus station." He said, "Okay, son." We both hung up the phone.

When I arrived in Houston on the Greyhound bus, I called my father and he picked me up at the bus station. In about twenty minutes, my father arrived at the bus station to pick me up. I saw my father when he pulled up at the bus station. I grabbed my bags and headed to his car. I put all my bags in my father's car and got in myself. My father asked me how had I been doing, since I moved with my Aunt Denise. I said, "Everything is fine, Daddy." He asked how were she and my cousins, Susan and Karen. I said, "They're all fine, too, Daddy." I asked my father how he had been doing. He said, "Okay. Just surviving."

I noticed that as we were approaching our exit off 610 that we didn't exit in our old neighborhood between Reed Rd. and Bellfort Blvd. on Alvin St. This was my father's residence a year ago. But rather, my father was exiting off 288 in Yellowstone Blvd. I thought maybe we were going to visit his sister-in-law, Jane Johnson. Well, when we got to Cullen Blvd., the light turned green and my dad kept straight through the light, passing by Finden St. where my Aunt Jane lived. So I was now wondering where were we going, since we already passed by her house. Then, my father told me plainly, "This is where I live now, son." My dad turned on Paris St. We arrived at his house and drove in the driveway. He said, "This is it. My new residence." I said, "Okay, Daddy. How long have you been here?" My father replied, "About eight months now."

I said, "Well, that's good, Daddy. Whatever happened to the well-known drug dealer who ran you out of your house?" My dad said, "They (the police) finally got them all." I said, "Good, Daddy! I'm glad you didn't go down with them, Daddy." My daddy said, "Yeah, I got out of that mess!" "It was crazy, Daddy," I said. "I was scared for your life. I didn't know what would happen to you due to your involvement with the well-known drug dealer. That day the police knocked on your door and was seeking for you, I became afraid for your freedom."

The police said, "I would like to speak to your father when he returns home." I thought this <u>could</u> not be true. However, it was very much so. Our house was being watched by the police. They were seeing all the traffic in and out of our house with a well-known drug dealer in Houston.

My father and I got out of his car and I grabbed all my bags. We went inside his house. We sat down in his house and my father asked me, "How was school?" I said, "School, is good, Daddy. In fact, my grades are better than last year." He said, "I'm proud of you, son. Keep up the good work! You will be fine. Are you working yet?" I said, "Yes sir, Daddy. I finally got my first legal job. My first legal job was at Taco Bell as a cashier but I have changed jobs since then. I now work at Krogers grocery store as a baggage clerk. I take out the customers' groceries. Daddy, I get paid minimum wages, $3.35 per hour, but it's better than nothing."

My daddy said, "At least you're working, son." I said, "Yes sir, Daddy. I like working, Daddy. I like receiving a legal paycheck. It feels great!" My daddy said, "I'm proud of you, son. Keep up the good work." I said, "I will, Daddy."

My father next asked me how my brother, Leroy was doing. I said, "Daddy, fine, but I haven't seen him since he went to Job Corps., out of town. The last time I saw Leroy was a year ago when we both were living here in Houston with you, Daddy." My father said, "Really!" I said, "Yes sir, Daddy." I got up and my father said, "You can sleep in this back room." I took my bags to the back room where I would sleep for a week or so. I visited my father for the majority of the Christmas holiday season. My father cooked me food the entire time I was visiting him. I got to visit with my Aunt Jane and her family during my stay there for the holiday season. I got to visit Mama Hodges, my father's second wife, and my older brothers who lived in Houston, too. I enjoyed them, as well, during my Christmas holiday season.

Well, the end of my time was nearing and I needed to be preparing for my departure back to Dallas. I gave everyone hugs and handshakes. I told my father that I loved him and that I would stay in contact with him more often. My father said, "That will be fine, son. Tell all your family hello there. You have a safe trip back to Dallas, and be careful. Call me when you make it to Dallas, okay? That way I will know that your trip was okay." I said, "Okay, Daddy, will do." I called the Greyhound bus station to confirm the next bus leaving for Dallas. I told my father what time it would be and he took out all my luggage. I told my father that I loved him and to take care. My father said the same, and I went inside the station to wait for my call for my bus to leave. In a while, they called over the intercom for my city to depart. I grabbed all my bags for the trip. I put all my bags on the bus and I got on. As I was leaving Houston, I felt a release in my spirit. I was able to visit my father and my other brothers and their mother. My father's health was fine, and above all my father was still looking okay. I was thankful for that!

In a few hours, I arrived back in Dallas, after having been gone for the majority of the Christmas holiday. I called my Aunt Denise to pick me up at the Greyhound bus station. I couldn't get an answer from her after calling multiple times, so I called C.B. to come pick me up, if he wasn't busy or didn't mind. C.B. asked me, "Why didn't you call your Aunt Denise to come pick you up from the bus station?" I told him that I had already called her multiple times without any response <u>whatsoever</u>. I told him this was strange, but I didn't know what was going on right now. "Just come get me, if you can." C.B. said, "Okay, I'll be there in a little while."

In about thirty minutes, C.B. showed up to pick me up. C.B. asked me again, "Have you heard anything yet?" I said, "No. I still don't have a clue whatsoever." So, C.B. and I were headed back to our neighborhood. Well, we got to my apartments. I got out of the car and he got out too, to assist me with all my bags. C.B. and I were taking my bags to the apartment where I lived with my Aunt Denise. I took out my key to the apartment, once I got to the top of the stairs. I put my key in the door, and I opened the door to learn that my Aunt

Raised From The Dead

Denise and her two daughters, Susan and Karen, had moved out without giving me any notice <u>whatsoever</u>.

No one told me anything concerning a move at all! The entire house was completely empty, except my property that was in the guest closet in the living room. I walked through the whole house to make sure of my speculation. Sure enough! They had all moved out. C.B. stayed at the front door in awe. He couldn't believe this had happened either. I thought, "This happens in movies and on TV, but not in real life." Well, I was so much wrong; it was my reality sure enough. I was seeing it, yet not believing it. It just couldn't be happening, I thought.

So after a while of losing my mind over this ordeal, I said, "Well, what do I do now, C.B.?" He said, "I don't know, brother. Let me talk to my mother." I said, "Okay. I appreciate whatever your mother can do. It would be a blessing." C.B. answered me back, "No problem! Whatever I can do to help you, brother." I said, "Thanks again!" C.B. and I both looked at one another again, not fully realizing why or how this could happen to me, while I was on my Christmas holiday vacation. All I could think in my mind was that this was what you call a "conspiracy," if there was ever such a word. My biological aunt did this to me, my mother's baby sister. I couldn't believe it.

Next, I asked C.B., "Where do I stay at tonight?" He said, "I don't know. Let me go talk to my mama and I be right back." I said, "Okay. I'll be right here." C.B.

left to go talk to his mother, in person. In about thirty minutes, C.B. returned to the apartment where I had been living. He said, "Grab all your property and let's go. I talked to my mama and she said that you could stay there with us for a couple of weeks until you find an apartment, or you might have to go back to Tyler." I said, "Thanks. Tell your mother thanks for me." He said, "I will." C.B. and I grabbed all my property and we put it in the back seat and trunk of his car.

C.B. let me keep all my property in the back of his car for a week, while we were going to school and work at the time. I thought I might see my cousin, Karen at school but I later learned she had transferred to the Magnet school with my cousin, Susan. It was so embarrassing to have all my property in his back seat for a whole week. C.B. and I were going from one apartment complex to the next, looking for the cheapest place for me to lay my head. We rode around for a week until we found a place called Club View Gardens Apartments. He and I went inside to talk to the leasing agent. I told him that I needed the cheapest thing that they had available today. The lady said, "We have an efficiency apartment available. Do you want it or not?" I said, "Yes ma'am. I'll take it." I asked the manager how much would the rent be there. She said $335, all bills paid. I thought about the numbers momentarily, and I said, "Yes ma'am, I'll take it. Please, don't let anyone else have it. I need it right away."

The manager next asked me did I have any apartment credit? I said, "No ma'am. I never have rented an apartment before." I then told her how I was living with my aunt and her two daughters and was basically put out in the streets. I told the apartment manager that I had no place to go, so I was desperately in need of a place to live. My Aunt Denise moved out of her apartment while I was on vacation visiting my father in Houston. After hearing my story, the manager requested a reference letter from my Aunt Denise. I told the lady manager that I would try to get one from her, but was not sure whether or not she would give me one on her credit. "Let me ask her," I replied. She said, "Here, take my card, call me at the office, and have your aunt call me too. Good luck!" I said, "Thanks, ma'am." She said, "No problem. I want to help." I said, "Thanks again." I left after receiving the card from her.

I called my Aunt Denise and thankfully she answered the phone. C.B. took me to my aunt's house to discuss this matter with her. We arrived at her new apartment. We went upstairs to chat with her about it. I knocked on the door. My Aunt Denise opened the door and greeted me with a hug as though nothing had ever happened. We hugged and C.B. hugged my Aunt Denise and spoke to her. My aunt invited us in her apartment. We sat down and she asked us what we needed. I thought to myself, "Really, I'm homeless!" I then told her that I was attempting to rent my own apartment, but I couldn't due to no rental history. I said, "Aunt Denise, I need a reference letter stating that you will verify about my job and work ethic and that I was living with you before seeking my own apartment." My aunt said, "Okay. I can do that for you, son. But you can't ruin my credit. You have to go to work and do whatever they tell you to do. You can't lose your job, son." I said, "Okay, Aunt. I won't." She said, "Okay. Give me a day or two to write this letter and discuss the matter with the apartment manager." I said, "Okay, Aunt Denise."

My aunt called the lady and discussed everything with her. They came to an agreement and gave me the apartment. My aunt called me and said, "The lady talked to me and afterwards decided to give you a chance. What the lady will give you is a six-month lease. I told the lady that I would be checking on you and assisting you, if needed." I said, "Okay. Thanks for giving her the letter and talking to the lady for me." I told the manager thanks too. The manager gave me a move in date. I told C.B. all about it. C.B. moved my belongings in with his car. So, C.B. and I got everything upstairs. I filled out all my apartment lease papers and moved in the very same day. Once I moved all my property in my room, I felt safe and secure again. My first apartment was an efficiency apartment. That's all I could afford, making $3.35 per hour. So, that's what I rented.

I thanked my best friend for all his assistance and concern for me as his friend. C.B. said, "No problem. If I were in your shoes, I think you would do it for me." I said, "Yes, I would, homey." C.B. and I chatted for a few more minutes and he went home for the night. I sat down and thought about my new living quarters and how I would survive at this point. I said to myself, "Well, I'm here, so I must keep going forward."

I started budgeting all my money. I would buy all generic food brands and save all the money possible. I worked hard at my job and studied even harder at school. I wanted to make good grades in school and I wanted to earn enough money to survive to pay my bills. Things were tough and rough on me, but I refused to give up, because I had C.B. Pruitt as my best friend. I felt that he was sent to me by God. The LORD Jesus Christ sent him to me. So, I felt confident if all else failed. He had proved to be a good and faithful friend early in friendship.

C.B. Pruitt was a teenage Christian and he would take me to church with him at times. I was encouraged very much to go forward and think positive as long as I had C.B. on my side. I did all my homework and made good grades, I think. I worked well at my job as a baggage clerk. I requested to work in the dairy for a while after being a baggage clerk. The dairy paid more money, so I went for it. I got the job to be a dairy stock worker. The dairy paid $3.65 per hour. I worked as a dairy stock worker for a while.

Then one day I went on break to the deli department for lunch. There was a young lady who went to Thomas Jefferson high school with me by the name of Sheila Baker. She was my cousin Susan's best friend. Well, Sheila rang me up some food from the deli department but didn't charge me correctly. She gave me a bogus receipt. The assistant manager came around the corner and looked in my plate. There was so much food, she became suspicious and asked to see my receipt. I gave it to her and she said, "Come with me, Lawrence." We went upstairs to the office. I told her that I was sorry about it. But she said, "You're fired." I said, "Ma'am, I really need my job." She said, "I'm sorry that's not my problem." I said, "Well, it will never happen again." She said, "No. Now, you have two options: you may resign or we can terminate you." I didn't understand, so she explained what each word meant. So I said, "Well, I guess I will resign." So, I resigned. The manager asked me to clock out and go home. She said, "You may come get your check on regular pay day schedule." I said okay.

I called C.B. about what had happened to me at work. I asked him what I should do next. He suggested that I put in a for a job at UPS. In a week or so I did exactly that. C.B. said, "They're hiring for college students and you have to be at least eighteen years of age." Luckily, I was already nineteen years old my senior year, so, I would meet the age requirement, if nothing else. So, in a week or so I went to UPS off Walnut Hill Lane and Monroe Dr. to fill out an application for a job. I went inside to inquire about the job for hire. A manager brought me an application and said, "Yes, we're hiring and you may fill out the application for the job now." I said, "Okay. Thank you, sir." He said, "No problem." I filled out the application and gave it to the man. The man said, "Do you have a contact number?" I told him, "No sir. But you may contact me through my best friends' phone number. My best friend's name is C.B. Pruitt. Or you may contact me by my Aunt Denise's phone number. Either way will be fine." He said, "Okay. I will give you a call after we check out everything."

In a couple of weeks, I was called back for a second interview. I had my interview and everything went swell. I was confident that I was about to get this job. But we still had one process waiting: it was called orientation. In about a week, I was called again for orientation for the job. We had the orientation at Ken's Pizza on Walnut Hill Lane. The orientation went swell. "Well," the manager said, "now, everyone who went through, be ready to work, because you have been hired from this point." The manager told us to be at work the following Monday at the twilight shift (5PM - 10PM). Everyone said okay. UPS offered $8 per hour to baggage clerks in the year 1989. I would be responsible for bagging, sorting by zip code and then placing packages on the conveyor belt for loading on the trucks.

I was so happy, I couldn't wait to tell everyone about my new job. I mean, I told my best friend first. Then I called my Aunt Denise and told her and I called my mama and told her. Then I called my father and told him. Everyone was glad for me and they thanked the Lord for me. I went from making $3.65per hour to making $8 per hour by just changing jobs to UPS as a loader and unloader in the warehouse. Life had already been better, changing from $3.35 to $3.65 per hour. Now, I would be making double the money by being hired by UPS. I started working the following Monday night as my new supervisor, Dennis Bagel, had said after orientation. I got to the job site. I learned my new job position and all my duties.

Our crew was only hired as seasonal workers. One day as the season was ending, my supervisor came to me after work and said, "Lawrence, I have been watching your work ethic and it's impressive." I said, "Thanks, Mr. Bagel" My supervisor said, "Hang around after work. I need to talk to you." I said, "Yes sir, Mr. Bagel."

Everyone else clocked out and went home. My supervisor said, "A lot of people are about to be cut, but we are going to keep a few good workers though, and you happen to be one of them." I said, "Thanks, Mr. Bagel! I really do appreciate that." He said, "So be encouraged when the season ends. Don't tell any of your co-workers what I just told you, okay?" I said, "Not a soul, Mr. Bagel. Thanks much!" I went home happy and thanking God, but not knowing Jesus Christ at the time. I told my best friend first of the good news, C.B. He was excited and happy for me. Then I told my Aunt Denise by phone and I called my mother.

Chapter 7

HOW WILL IT ALL END?

In the year 1989, I graduated from Thomas Jefferson High in Dallas. My Mama came from Tyler, Texas to attend my graduation from high school. My cousin, Karen and my brother, Leroy, all attended my graduation. Leroy took all my graduation pictures the night of my graduation. Clarence, my best friend and I both graduated together and took pictures together after graduation the same night. After all my set-backs and disappointments of changing schools and failing my sixth grade year and my ninth grade year, here I was walking across the stage, receiving a high school graduation diploma.

My final two years of high school, I attended school in Dallas. I could not believe this day had arrived, because I wanted to be a drop-out a few years back. I thank my Lord and Savior, Jesus Christ, for making this day possible for me. If it hadn't been for the Lord Jesus Christ, I would not have graduated, period.

This is what I call the grace of God at work in a person's life. The Lord Jesus Christ was continuing to open doors in my life and continuing to work on my behalf. Graduating from high school was an extraordinary event for a wannabe drop-out. I could not even imagine such an event being true. I give all the glory, praise and honor to my personal Lord and Savior, Jesus Christ, for allowing such an event to happen in my life.

The seasonal lay-off from UPS came around but I stayed just as my supervisor, Dennis Bagel had said. I continued to work hard as before. I even worked harder after he kept me. In the course of time, my supervisor came to me again with a proposition of promotion. He said, "Lawrence, would you like to work on the line in the back as a sorter instead of a baggage clerk?" I said, "Yes sir." The supervisor said, "I will give you a test. You take your time and study the test. If you pass, we will make you a sorter and you will be making an extra dollar, $9 per hour." I took all the material to study for the sorting job for a couple of weeks, then I told him that I was ready for the sorting test. He said, "Okay. Give me a few days to set up everything and I will have you come in and take the test." I said okay.

A few days passed by and my supervisor said: "Are you ready?" I said, "Yes sir!" He gave me the test and I passed it! My supervisor said, "Just as I thought, Lawrence, you would pass the test." I said, "I studied hard for it, sir." He said, "Good job! I'm proud of you!" I said, "Thanks a lot!" Now I was making $9 per hour and life was even better, because I had an extra dollar raise added to my hourly wages. I worked hard and learned all my duties as a sorter. I did a great job as a sorter.

Then, in the course of time, I met a guy at UPS by the name of Kurt, who was a sorter. Kurt and I got acquainted with one another before and after work. He was a Christian man. He would tell me about Jesus Christ at times. He also would listen to Christian music. He would attempt to ask me to go to church with him. But I would reject the offer. Kurt would offer me a ride to and from work at times, as a Christian. Now, I didn't turn down the ride to and from work because I was tired of walking already, so the ride was fitting for me. So, I accepted the rides whenever he offered them to me. Kurt and I became friends after a while. He and I both put in another application to work for RNA Freight System unloading trucks. We both went in together to fill out our applications. We filled them out and turned them in together. We both got called in for an interview for the part-time job. They offered to pay us $12.70 per hour to work part-time loading eighteen-wheeler trucks, only on the weekends.

Kurt and I both started working the job at RNA Freight System and we learned all our job duties and responsibilities. By Kurt and me working a second job together, we now had an opportunity to bond even more together. In the course of time, C.B. Pruitt and I had a discussion about working for a trucking

Raised From The Dead

company by the name of Welch Motor Lines. C.B. and I went to the company to inquire about the job. They said, "Yes, we're hiring. Would you like to fill out an application now or take it with you?" I said, "Sir, may I fill out one now?" He said, "Yes, that will be fine." I said, "Okay."

He brought me an application and I filled it out. When I gave the application back to him, he said, "We will call you in a few days or so for an interview." I said, "Thanks! Have a great day, sir!" I left the building afterwards. In a week or so, the manager called both C.B. and me in for an interview for the job. C.B. and I both got the job. He and I both were excited about the job at Welch Motor Lines. I told my Aunt Denise by phone about my third job. I called my mother and told her about the job at Welch Motor Lines. I called my father about my new job too. Welch offered to pay us $6.50 per hour, to work unlimited hours. C.B. and I both worked the same shift since we were able to make our own schedule. C.B. and I learned all our duties and responsibilities in loading the truck. Life was good and I was making good and honest money working for a living.

Then, one day I met a young man by the name of Danny Drucker. Danny went to Thomas Jefferson High School with me. Danny was a drug dealer. He had a proposal for me, to take my hard working and honest money and invest it into drugs. Danny said, "You're working all those jobs and making all that money. Would you like to make money from your

How Will It All End?

own money? All you have to do is buy the drugs with your money and I will sell them for you and we will split the profit."

Danny explained to me how to make a profit off my own money by investing. I told him to let me think on it for a couple of days, then I would get back with him. He said, "Okay, but it's easy money. All you will be doing is investing your money like a bank and receive your interest after I sell all the product (drugs, crack cocaine)." I said, "Okay. Still, I need to think about it for a few days, or so."

Derrick and I went our separate ways. After thinking on the subject for a few days, I was thinking, after all, I don't have to touch anything except cash money and receive a profit by just investing my legal money. I could give it a try and see what happened, I told myself. I called Danny back by his beeper and told him, "Let's meet to discuss the matter, in person." He said, "Okay. Let's meet outside my apartment and we can go somewhere in private to discuss the matter." I said, "Okay." I picked up him at his apartment and we went to a nearby lake and discussed the matter there. We agreed to split whatever the profit was after he had made the $500 that I had invested. I gave him the $500 cash. I told him to take care of business and call me when he finished. He said, "Okay." I took him back home.

In a few days or so, Danny called me back and said, "I got your $500 back. Now, I'm working on our profit that we will divide evenly between the two of us." I said, "Okay. I appreciate it. Thanks for not lying to me about my money." Danny said, "I told you everything was okay." I said, "Okay. Well we're in business, now." In a few more days, Danny called me and said, "I have the rest of the money." I said, "How much?" He said, "Another $500, so we will divide it evenly." So, I made $250 in a week or so. All I had to do was invest my legal money and Danny sold all the drugs by himself. So, I became an investor for profit and a supplier of drugs.

In the course of time, I was arrested for first degree murder because I was a witness to the shooting death of an individual. I went to jail Feb. 26, 1991, and made bond for $25,000. I stayed in jail two days. While I was in jail, I was thinking, "I didn't kill nor shoot the deceased. Why am I here?" However, deep in my heart, I knew more about the case and I felt more involved than others had thought because I was an investor in a drug business. I was thinking that the investment in this drug business had landed me in jail.

My Aunt Denise found me an trial attorney in Dallas while I was still in jail. My brothers, Leroy and Perry came to visit me in jail and said, "You need $2,500 to get you bonded out of jail." I told him to call Stacy from Garland, TX. Stacy was one of my customers from the drug deals. I told Stacy to lend me $2,500 to get bonded out of jail and I would reimburse him later. Stacy said, "Put your car up for collateral until I get my money back." I told him okay. My brothers,

Perry and Leroy, took Stacy my Cadillac for collateral. Stacy kept my car for two days and gave my brothers the $2,500 for my bond money. My brothers took the money to the bail bondsmen and they released me from jail on a $25,000 bond. I gave Stacy his $2,500 back immediately to get back my car. He handed me my Cadillac keys. I told Stacy thanks for the favor. I appreciated it very much. He said, "No problem."

My aunt heard that I had been released from jail on bond. She said she wanted to see me. I said, "Okay, Aunt Denise. I will be there shortly." I went to her house to discuss the release and attorney matters with her. When I arrived at my aunt's house, she said, "I see you have gotten yourself in trouble. What's going on?" I wouldn't tell my aunt what was going on because she didn't raise me this way, so I was embarrassed. So I just told her that I had got in trouble for no reason whatsoever. My aunt didn't believe me, of course. However, I did tell her that I was involved in drugs, but not a user, just a seller. My Aunt Denise started telling me about the trial attorney that she selected for me and asked me to call him about my court date. My aunt provided me with all the trial attorney's information on a business card.

I called the attorney and asked him about my case. He told me to come to his office for an appointment with him. Then I resumed discussing this matter with my Aunt Denise. I told her that I had just made an appointment with the trial attorney and I would be visiting him shortly. She said, fine. My aunt decided to change the subject and talk about the Bible. She started telling me that Jesus loved me and that He wanted to be a part of my life. I said, "Thanks for the offer." My aunt asked me if I had a Bible to read. I told her, "NO," so she provided me with one of hers. I took the Bible but I felt that I was going to continue in my current lifestyle of being part of selling drugs.

Days that followed after my Aunt Denise gave one of her Bibles, she started telling me about reading the Psalms. I didn't know where that book was in the Bible at the time. My aunt showed it to me in the Bible and she specifically told me to learn Psalm 23 and learn it verbatim. My aunt said, "It's only six verses," so I learned it by heart. I took the Bible that my aunt gave me and put it in the back window of my yellow Cadillac, but I never opened it up until my court date.

The court date arrived and I opened my Bible. I had marked Psalm 23 with a piece of paper. The trial started and then I picked up my Bible and read it in my car on my very first court date. I read it again upstairs even though I didn't quite understand it. I prayed to Jesus but was not a Christian and had no knowledge of what I was doing. All I knew was that my Aunt Denise said, "Read your Bible and trust in Jesus Christ." So I was trying to do what she asked me concerning religion because I wanted help.

I still didn't know whether Jesus Christ was the correct way to turn or not, but I said to myself, "I guess

I can give it a try." I had tried the wrong way with drugs, it didn't work, so Jesus was worth a try. I began reading Psalm 23, but nothing was really clear to me at the time, due to my lack of knowledge and wisdom. I read it and read it until I learned the six verses verbatim, yet lacked what the word of God was saying to me. I continued to go to court and read just Psalm 23. This was all my Aunt Denise asked me to read and learn. So I did just that.

During the trial days, I began to read Psalms 23 at least once a day. I did this every day for five days.

Meanwhile my mother, kept telling me to trust in the lord Jesus Christ, "He will take care of you." Finally, after going to court Monday through Friday every day of the week, my court day came on that Saturday morning. Yes, on a Saturday morning about 9 AM. The judge found me guilty of first degree murder and gave me a life sentence under the 1/4 Law on October 19, 1991 in Dallas County, Texas. I cried and told my mother that I loved her and to take my keys and told her where my car was parked in the jail parking lot. My mother took my keys and the bailiffs took me into custody to start my long-term sentence for first degree murder.

My Life continues in Book 2 –
''When Miracles Began" (2006)
Available soon in both print and ebook!

MY MESSAGE TO YOU THE READER

WHAT DID I LEARN THROUGH THIS EXPERIENCE AND HOW CAN I GLORIFY JESUS CHRIST THROUGH IT?

Well, first of all, I must acknowledge Jesus Christ is the resurrection and He has power to bring the dead back to life. Next, I can and will bring glory to Jesus Christ by testifying about how He raised me from the dead and how I am continuing to live my life for Him. In addition, this experience brought me into a closer personal relationship with Jesus Christ and gave me a godly fear that I wouldn't have had without it. I took more chances with sin before this event happened. This experience proved to me that Jesus Christ evidently still has work for me to do here on earth.

I learned through this experience that:

- Jesus Christ shows grace even to those that do wrong.
- All things work together for good to those who love God and are called according to His purpose.
- Jesus Christ is merciful and gracious.
- Jesus Christ sustained my life on Tuesday (first day of symptoms of Brugada Syndrome), Wednesday, and Thursday morning.
- Jesus Christ resurrects and sustains life to whomever He chooses.
- Jesus Christ works by numbers today just as He did in the Bible.
- Jesus Christ is omniscient, omnipresent, and omnipotent.

I believe that Jesus Christ knew Satan's plan and allowed him to carry it out, knowing that He had a backup plan. I believe each saint has an assigned angel, and mine was definitely watching over me on Thursday, September 26, 2013.

To whom it may concern.

If you would like to call or text me by cell phone or email me for any questions about my book or testimony: you may call me at my cell phone number below:

(972) 607-5056 or email me at: lawrencehodges29@yahoo.com

My Message to You the Reader

It's my pleasure to answer any questions concerning my book.

May the Lord bless you in Jesus' name!

Lawrence Hodges

ABOUT THE AUTHOR

God's work can be subtle, or it can be dramatic and life altering

On September 26, 2013 Lawrence Hodges had no pulse and no breath for 15 minutes. God brought him back to learn the reason for his terrifying attack: Brugada syndrome. His life was forever changed by the very likely chance he will experience another, possibly fatal, heart attack—at any time.

This is not the first test God had placed before Lawrence.

Years before, as a young man, he was headed down a path of gambling, violence, and theft. Trying desperately to find what was missing in his life, he continued to trust the wrong people and eventually found himself in prison facing a life sentence for murder. It was there, at his lowest point, where he finally found God and began studying His word.

Now, facing a diagnosis of Brugada syndrome, he must trust God to show him how to live as a survivor and come to terms with his new condition both physically and spiritually. In this autobiography, Lawrence reveals his journey to God and how His word has saved him, body and soul.

CPSIA information can be obtained
at www.ICGtesting.com
Printed in the USA
FSOW01n1802160216
17022FS